SEEING
BIRMINGHAM
BY TRAM

1906

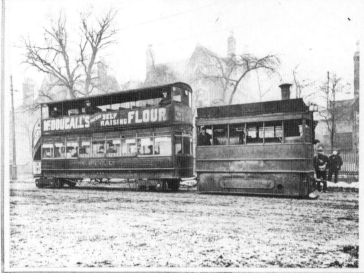

PAST AND PRESENT

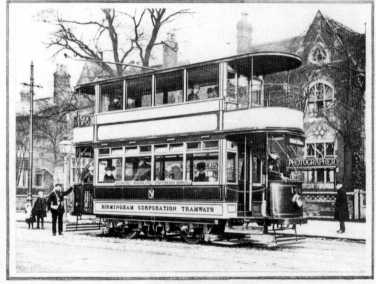

1907

This well presented card is symbolic of the watershed in tram development that had been reached. To the PRESENT could be added, with hindsight, the FUTURE as the overhead electric tramway system lasted until 1953.

SEEING BIRMINGHAM BY TRAM

Eric Armstrong

TEMPUS

Horse-drawn trams plodded into use in Nechells during 1884. This service, operated by the City of Birmingham Tramways Co., ran between Albert Street (city centre) and Butlin Street, Nechells, a distance of about two miles. Apparently, the value of mobile advertising 'hoardings' had already been recognised!

First published 2003

Tempus Publishing Limited
The Mill, Brimscombe Port,
Stroud, Gloucestershire, GL5 2QG

© Eric Armstrong 2003

The right of Eric Armstrong to be identified as the Author
of this work has been asserted by him in accordance with the
Copyrights, Designs and Patents Act 1988.

British Library Cataloguing in Publication Data.
A catalogue record for this book is available from the British Library.

ISBN 0 7524 2787 3

Typesetting and origination by Tempus Publishing Limited
Printed in Great Britain by Midway Colour Print, Wiltshire

Contents

Acknowledgements

In carrying out the research required for this book I warmly acknowledge the help I have received from the following sources:

Bunce, J.T. et al, *History of the Corporation of Birmingham* (Birmingham Corporation)

Clegg, Chris and Rosemary, *The Dream Palaces of Birmingham* (Chris and Rosemary Clegg, 1983)

Collins, Paul, *Birmingham Corporation Transport 1904-1939* (Ian Allan Publishing, 1999)

 – *Birmingham Corporation Transport 1939-1969* (Ian Allan Publishing, 1999)

Jones, Douglas V., *The Story of Erdington* (The Westwood Press, 1995)

Marks, John, *Birmingham on Old Postcards*, (Reflections of a Bygone Age: Vol.1, 1982; Vol.2, 1983; Vol.3 1990)

 – *Birmingham Trams on Old Picture Postcards* (Reflections of a Bygone Age, 1992)

Price, Victor J. *Handsworth Remembered* (Brewin Books, 1992)

Turner, Keith, *Birmingham Pubs* (Tempus, 1999)

Various old Ordnance Survey maps published by Alan Godfrey Maps.

The following photographers' names appear on the backs of photographs: W.A. Camwell; R.B. Parr; R.J.S. Wiseman; Jack Mellor; John H. Meredith; M.J. O'Connor, and others with blurred initials: A.S.D?, H.T.W.?, P.W.W.?

Additions to captions, in italics, are extracts from my schoolboy diaries of 1938, 1939 and 1940. During this three-year period, I grew from being an impressionable fourteen-year-old to a still more impressionable seventeen-year-old.

Introduction

For more than forty years the sharp, metallic ping ping of a warning bell and a distinctive gliding swish were familiar sounds along many of Birmingham's busy thoroughfares. Trams were on the move. Electric trams, that is, which provided an efficient and praiseworthy public transport service from 1907 to 1953.

Birmingham's overhead wire electric trams, when introduced in 1907, were regarded by many local people as a wonder of the age. By the time the last tram made its final journey, to Erdington in 1953, people were generally more blasé about technological advances than their parents and grandparents had been.

Even so, the farewell swish and the final pings of the last trams were accompanied by affectionate cheering crowds who lined the 'funeral' routes to applaud a good job well done.

But the story of Birmingham's trams begins much earlier than 1907, reaching as far back as 1874. Tramway routes, from initial short filaments, grew into complex, city-wide, spider web-shaped networks only to be dismantled over time as bus services gained the ascendancy.

It is fitting to look briefly at the background history of those eight decades, 1874-1953. During that period generations of British people experienced dramatic and far-reaching changes.

In the age of the steam tram, and a powerful British Empire, two Boer Wars in South Africa were fought. Later followed two world wars and finally the Korean War. Between the two world wars most British people had to battle with economic depression and high unemployment. But, without doubt, the man in the street in 1953 was economically and socially far better off than his counterpart had been in 1874. So were his wife and children. Votes for women and the establishment of the Welfare State had contributed greatly to the making of a much fairer society.

An 1874 tram passenger could not know that Queen Victoria was still to reign for another quarter of a century. In 1874 her son, later King Edward VII, met 'the radical republican mayor of Birmingham', Joseph Chamberlain. Two miners were elected to the House of Commons. Disraeli, the prime minister, pushed through an Act to ensure that no child below ten years of age could be employed in a textile factory. Quite a different world from that of 1953.

1953 brought the 'Matthews Cup Final', the first and British successful ascent of Mount Everest and the Coronation of Queen Elizabeth II. Sweet rationing ended (eight years after the end of the war), British POWs arrived home from Korea, Joseph Stalin died and the England cricket team won back the Ashes after a lapse of twenty years.

Throughout the seventy-eight-year period of tram transport, Birmingham grew appreciably as a city. This was partly due to the influx of people seeking work in a city soundly based economically and offering '1,001 trades' in which to seek employment. Additionally, the incorporation of neighbouring parishes such as Handsworth, Aston and Northfield also played an important part in the city's growth. So with the expansion of the city in population and area came the need to expand first its tramway, then its bus service. Furthermore, as old houses were replaced with new, housing estates, some private, many municipal, sprang up in leafier suburbs and on Greenfield sites, but all requiring public transport.

Tram routes were extended to serve some of these estates while for others, such as Kingstanding and Perry Common, only bus services were provided. Some tram services were extended to carry workers to new factories being built in the outer suburbs as part of main road ribbon development, such as Dunlop's move from Aston to a location near the Chester Road.

While the historical context and background remain important, the essential purpose of this book is to pay tribute to the Birmingham tram and its associated staff, from the perspective of one of its millions of past passengers. The approach adopted therefore is not one of detailed history or paying close attention to technical matters to do with trams and track as engineering products. Without ignoring the above factors, the emphasis is squarely placed on the tram in its scenic context – what a would-be passenger, passenger or bystander might see and remember.

Where photographs, mostly postcards, do not depict a tram, the illustrations are closely related to the reasons why a passenger may be undertaking a particular tram journey. In my opinion, this is how the Brummie tram passenger, from no matter what part of the city, would probably best recognise and remember his or her journey to work, to school, a visit to the cinema, a shopping trip to town, cheering on the Villa, Birmingham City or the 'Baggies'.

Having decided on the general approach outlined above, I thought that the best and simplest method of arranging the photographs was by following the various tram routes, one route at a time. So, the postcards shown are basically in tram stop order, if not in time sequence order.

The year 1937 for tram routes in operation was chosen for a number of reasons. Despite the growth of the bus services, trams still operated in all parts of the city except the south-east sector, which included Hall Green and Acocks Green. Not until the financial year 1936-1937 did the number of bus passengers (190,464,952) exceed that of tram passengers (186,576,388). So the routes for 1937 seemed sufficiently extensive to portray a city's network in a reasonably representative manner. According to the official timetable for the year (see page 31) thirty-three routes were in operation, that figure including five that were for 'rush periods only'.

Of course, relatively few of the tram scenes shown in the book date from 1937. But I don't think that matters greatly because time travellers, as any nostalgia buffs must be, can readily step down from a tram in a 1939 scene to board one from 1907 or 1952.

Diagrams of the different routes are presented very roughly in the manner of a compass, starting at a setting of north-north-west and working round in a clockwise direction.

While the book concentrates on tram rides, the personnel who made such rides possible, day after day and in all weathers, have not been overlooked. Neither has the point that trams need somewhere to 'rest up' to be maintained and repaired. So, photographs of depots, workshops and men at work have been included. So have 'special occasions' such as Coronation celebrations in which trams formed a notable and popular element.

Conceivably every type of transport generates its own distinctive ambience and I readily confess that riding on a tram gave me far more pleasure than a bus ride. For one thing, there were no petrol or diesel fumes to contend with, no crashing of gears or noisy revving sounds. By comparison, the supply of power to the tram was almost silent, a mere background whisper.

Visually, all around the inside of the tram, on both decks, pleasing testimony to the craftsman joiner's skills was on display in the panelling and ceiling, the heavy slide across wooden doors. A passenger could almost sense the layer upon layer of varnish being applied by dedicated workers.

Then there were the little personal experiences shared with many. Let me recall a few: the lengthwise (as distinct from crosswise) wooden seats on some trams which, if not fully occupied, could cause passengers to slide up and down the seats according to the gradient on which the tram was travelling and its speed; the territorial rights exercised at each end of some trams (see page 35) where the vestibules, though roofed, remained partly open at the sides. The seating here could, at times, be monopolised by a gaggle of schoolgirls, chattering like starlings, or a group of schoolboys ragging one another. In either case, the heavy wooden doors would be drawn to, thus keeping at bay the tiresome 'aliens' in the main compartment. How many of us can recall the rapid rock and roll progress along stretches of the Bristol Road where, almost invariably, drivers caused the tram to sway from side to side?

But the terminus has been reached, a rhythmic thud, thud, thud can be heard as the reversible seats are turned 'the other way' for the return journey.

Enough! 'Tickets please – and pass along the car.'

One
Early Days

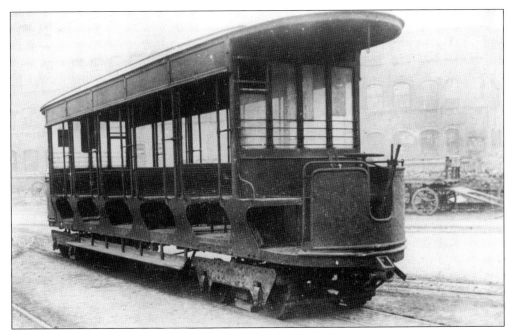

This early cable car relied on a simple form of technology (see next page) and the vehicle itself could hardly be more basic as regards passenger and driver comfort. It is thought that the photograph was taken at the Hockley tram depot.

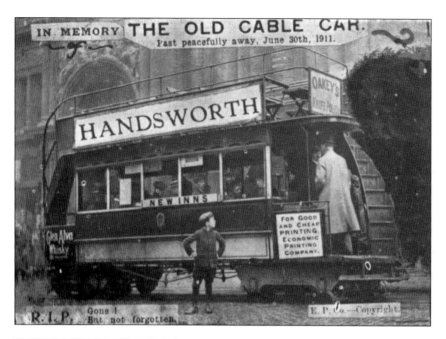

IN MEMORY THE OLD CABLE CAR.
Past peacefully away, June 30th, 1911.

HANDSWORTH

OAKEY'S KNIFE POLISH

NEW INNS

FOR GOOD AND CHEAP PRINTING. ECONOMIC PRINTING COMPANY.

R.I.P.   Gone !
But not forgotten.

E. P. Co.—Copyright.

NEW ST. & LONDON L.&N.W.R.
40 TRAINS DAILY 40

HARRY SMITH   SCREW PINS   Reckitt's Blue

CABLE CAR'S FAREWELL.

Farewell, kind friends, I'm going
   To the scrap heap, so they say ;
The worthy City Fathers
   Think too long I've held the sway.
They deem me old and ugly,
   In fact, not up to date :
If ever love they had for me
   Their love's turned into hate.

This city's known as " Forward "—
   A motto that means well ;
'Tis that what makes them anxious
   The cable car to sell.
Some say that I'm not handsome,
   But most of them agree
When electric cars they take my place
   Improvement there will be.

And now before I leave you
   Kind friends take my advice :
And you, both guards and drivers
   Who all have acted nice—
Give out a hearty welcome
   When the new friend does appear ;
For though his name's Electric Car
   To your welfare he's sincere

Composed by John Bryan.

Above: The cable car, introduced in 1886-1887, was so called because of the continuously moving cable, set in a slot on the road, to which the tram could be attached and released by a claw or 'gripper' mechanism. In 1888 Colmore Row was linked with Hockley by this means and a year later the route was extended to New Inns, Handsworth, remaining in use until 1911. The system was first tried in San Francisco in 1873.

Left: Early postcard publishers were quick to realise the sales opportunities afforded by interesting events. Whatever the merits of the poem, the top deck advertisement provides a startling reminder of how efficient steam train services could be, nearly a century ago.

Steam trams made their debut in Birmingham in 1884. The tram comprised two vehicles: a steam locomotive and a tram car without power. This photograph *c.*1888 is thought to show the Spon Lane tram shed in West Bromwich. Rudimentary concern for safety and comfort is illustrated by the 'cow catcher' on the loco and the vestibule, sheltering passengers against fumes and smoke, on the upper deck of the car.

In addition to the Kitson loco, Falcon and Beyer Peacock locomotives were also used for traction purposes. One can imagine a wag making witty use of the Mellin's advert 'for INFANTS and INVALIDS' as the tram laboured up a taxing incline! Borax (see top deck of tram) is a salt with antiseptic properties and, years ago, was used for gargling purposes.

This photograph is thought to have been taken c.1900. In addition to Aston, other steam tram routes were introduced as follows: Moseley Road 1884; Kings Heath 1887; Perry Barr 1884; Witton 1884; Lozells 1884 and Saltley 1884. An officially appointed historian of the time lamented: 'In the year 1900 the steam-trams were still running on nearly all the lines of the City to the disgust of the inhabitants and the amazement of visitors'.

This humorous card could be readily overprinted with the routes and towns wherever steam trams operated. This card was posted in Skegby, Mansfield, in 1914 to someone who presumably had memories of rides on Birmingham steam trams.

In Remembrance of

THE BIRMINGHAM & DISTRICT OLD STEAM TRAMS

WHICH STARTED SERVICE NOVEMBER 25th, 1884.

PASSING AWAY OWING TO AN ELECTRIC SHOCK JANUARY 1st, 1907.

"Let not ambition mock their useful toils,
Their homely joys and destiny obscure."

Photo by]   [P. King.

This card was posted in Hockley on 31 January 1907. A city dweller aunt writes to her country town (Malvern) nephew: 'I thought you would like this PC. They are the latest [to] come out.' The quotation is from a poem that would have been familiar to many contemporary children, namely Thomas Gray's *Elegy in a Country Churchyard*, which begins with the familiar line: 'The curfew tolls the knell of parting day'.

Starting in 1888-1890 unsuccessful attempts were made to develop trams powered by electric accumulators. 1901 brought the introduction of overhead electric wiring, a traction method 'universally' adopted in 1907. By this time, various tramway routes had been taken over by the City of Birmingham Tramways. The gauge of 3ft 6in (narrower than the standard railway gauge) had earlier become the norm. So, things were in place for a city-wide system of public tram transport to be built. But on the evidence of the card, there was still some way to go regarding the comfort of top deck passengers – and the staff.

This forty-eight-seater has been photographed inside a depot *c*.1904/1905. Staff uniforms now seem to be established. The man on the left may be an inspector or supervisor of some kind. Level with his right arm runs an advert for 'Bryant & May's Matches'. The driver now enjoys better protection from the elements but not the passengers 'on top'.

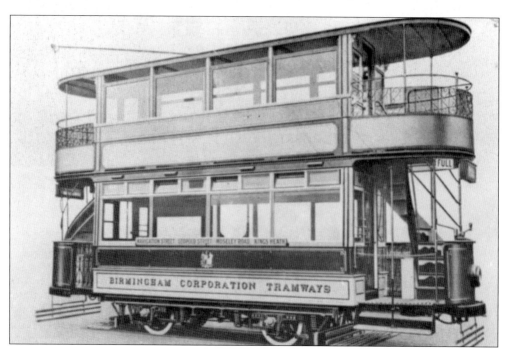

Right: While Birmingham had been a self-governing town since 1838, the grant of city status in 1889 prompted the adoption of a new coat of arms. This depicted industry (the blacksmith) and art (a lady holding an artist's palette). The motto, appropriate to the city's hardworking, industrial character was 'Forward'.

The shape of things to come is illustrated here. The No.44 tram route from Dale End in the city was extended in 1922 to the junction of Warwick Road and Westley Road, Acocks Green. The bus shown, the 1A route, had completely replaced the tram service by 1937. The photograph dates from 1929. As a boy aged six at the time, I remember the ladies' fashionable cloche hats and the uncovered bus staircase.

Opposite below: This pristine, showroom-condition tram is apparently destined for the Navigation Street, Leopold Street, Moseley Road, King's Heath route. The car clearly displays Birmingham's coat of arms, conferred on the new city in 1889. By 1912 the Corporation owned sixty route miles of electric tramway. Each tram averaged a daily run of some eighty-four miles, with passengers for the year numbering 113 million.

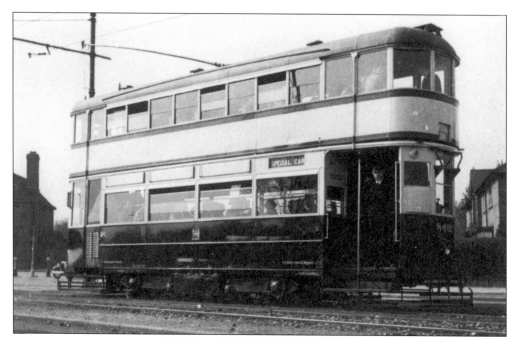

This state-of-the-art (1948) tramcar has been photographed at the start of a stretch of reserved track in Bordesley Green East. Five years later trams had vanished from Birmingham's streets.

A common problem, but one especially acute on Saturday evenings: how many passengers can be allowed on the last tram? No doubt this type of card, suitably overprinted, could sell well in any community with a tram service. This card was posted in Birmingham on 21 August 1907.

Two

North-North-Western and Northern Routes

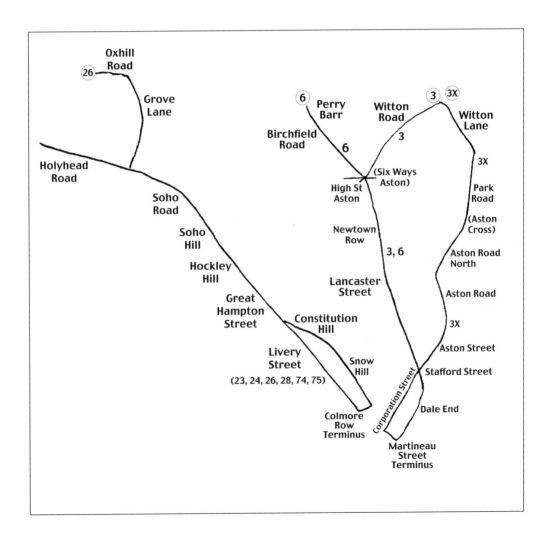

Oxhill Road
26
Grove Lane
Holyhead Road
Soho Road
Soho Hill
Hockley Hill
Great Hampton Street
Livery Street
(23, 24, 26, 28, 74, 75)
Constitution Hill
Snow Hill
Colmore Row Terminus

6
Perry Barr
Birchfield Road
6
High St Aston
(Six Ways Aston)
Newtown Row
Lancaster Street

Witton Road
3
3, 6

3   3X
Witton Lane
3X
Park Road
(Aston Cross)
Aston Road North
Aston Road
3X
Aston Street
Stafford Street
Corporation Street
Dale End
Martineau Street Terminus

The New Inns Handsworth Scott Series Nº 1085

As no overhead wiring can be seen, the photograph presumably shows a cable car which ran on this route until 1911 (see page 10). The New Inns Hotel was a major landmark on the Holyhead Road and for many years was Handworth's premier location for a 'bit of a do', the hotel possessing both a banqueting hall and a ballroom.

This similar scene probably dates from the 1920s, with electric tram services well established. In 1937 services from Colmore Row to Dudley (74) and Wednesbury (75) passed along this way. During 'rush periods' the 28 would also travel from Colmore Row to New Inns, which had earlier formed the boundary for services from the Black Country.

But a short distance apart on the Holyhead and Soho Roads, two cinemas undoubtedly swelled tram passenger numbers, especially on Saturday evenings. The Albion opened during the First World War (1916) and was later enlarged to appear as it does in the photograph.

During the 1930s the Regal was one of Birmingham's most prestigious cinemas. Opened in 1929 with a 'talkies' programme, it could seat over 2,000 film fans, although it may be wondered how many went to see *Four Men and a Prayer*.

Saturday 6 May 1939. Feel on top of the world. Saw Margaret at night and we went to the Regal and saw The Citadel. *1/3 seats. Celebrating.* (My success at school sports).

19

Soho Road comprised a long and very busy thoroughfare. The unusual width of the pavement, right, allowed throngs of jostling shoppers to make headway. Some bargain hunters would plunge into the indoor Handsworth Market, noisy and entertaining, especially when crockery sellers were in full raucous cry. In the distance, left, rises the clock tower of Handsworth Council House. (Handsworth was once a UDC).

Thursday 6 April 1939. Went to Handsworth Market...to buy some eggs for Mom. Heckled the quack medicine sellers. Great fun.

This view towards New Inns shows part of a shopping area lying between Rookery Road and Grove Lane. Many of the shops were branches of local or national retailers, e.g. Dewhurst, butchers; Baines, bakers; Burtons, tailors; Woolworths and Boots. During the 1930s, Saturday, and sometimes other evenings, would bring about a pre-courtship ritual, long abandoned. Young adolescents, usually in pairs of the same sex, would stroll up and down the 'monkey run' seeking to strike up flirtatious conversations with a view to romance.

Saturday 5 February 1938. Went out with Allan at night. Found two decent bits of fluff.
('Decent' referred to appearance).

20

A few yards further on, towards town, the names of two other major retailers appear. A hoarding occupies the intervening gap to advertise the film *In Old Chicago*, showing at The Albion (page 19). This film, released in 1938, starred Tyrone Power and Alice Faye, the story being based on the great fire that nearly destroyed Chicago in 1871. Reputedly this fire was started by a Mrs O'Leary's cow which accidentally kicked over a lantern and the rest was – conflagration!

Many postcards feature this fine redbrick seat of local government. For many years Handsworth formed part of Staffordshire before being incorporated into Birmingham in 1911. The building housed not only council meeting rooms but an art school and a library. The sheep crossing the road constitute an interesting aspect of the scene.

The sender of the card, posted on 1 September 1938, writes: 'the weather is cooling down here now and our Winter trade in Radio is just starting to get busy...'. The radio shop can be seen on the right. Stafford Road runs left behind the boy, and part of the pub, The Frighted Horse, can be seen on the corner.

This type of tram, which ran from Colmore Row, is close to its terminus at Stafford Road. Around 1914 the service was subsequently designated the 23 (Handsworth and Colmore Row 'rush periods only' 1937) (see page 31). The corner position of The Frighted Horse is now clearer.

'Dear Mother, I am getting short of Cheese, if Uncle will take 60s I should be glad if you would rail me 5 or 6…' So wrote George Lawton, grocer, of 78 Soho Road on 8 June 1909. The Stores, well stocked with whisky and summer bedding plants, also offered home farm eggs for sale.

Moving towards town, Soho Road becomes Soho Hill which the cable car is about to descend. Sloping down to the left is Villa Road along which services 5 (Lozells, Slade Road, Gravelly Hill) and 24 (Lozells and Colmore Row (via Wheeler Street)) would eventually travel (see page 31). The tram shown would pass through Hockley to Colmore Row.

23

The tram has just reached the top of Livery Street and is about to turn into Colmore Row where it will arrive at its terminus by the railway station entrance. Elderly Brummies may recall that a common description for a person in a grumpy mood was: 'he's got a face on him as long as Livery Street.'

In this later photograph taken on 31 March 1939, a tram on the Dudley route is close to journey's end. Birmingham city centre's controversial one-way traffic system was now in place and perhaps unfairly derided. But the 'No Entry' sign did not apply to the six tram services using Livery Street and Colmore Row.

Another of the various tram services to travel along the Soho Road into the city was the No.26, shown here at its suburban terminus in Oxhill Road, Handsworth. This photograph, taken in 1939, shows Belisha beacons in place at the entrance to Rookery Road. The beacons derive their name from Mr Hore-Belisha who, as Minister of Transport, introduced them along with other road safety measures including the driving test.

This photograph, taken from the corner of Windermere Road, looks towards the tram terminus. The newspaper placards include some interesting headlines, for example: 'Xmas Gift Books for your Children', 'Mystery of Injured Cyclist in Church' and 'Will There be Another War?' That question suggests that the scene is one from December 1937 or 1938.

Saturday 23 November1940. Felt like something the cat had dragged in at work. Had to make detours. Bombs Oxhill Road, Island Road. Terrible damage. No water or gas. First parade with Home Guard. (While the parade was hardly one of the turning points of the war, it made me feel a lot better!)

'The Grove' refers to the Ansells pub (built 1891) on the left-hand corner of Grove Lane where the tram has just turned into Oxhill Road. A stretch of dual carriageway, although short in this instance, was relatively rare in older suburbs. The card was posted in August 1927. Bearing left ahead is College Road, while to the right runs Church Lane.

'Boulevard' seems just a little grand for the dual carriageway concerned. But perhaps it raised local self esteem and property values? The sign fastened to the first pole appears to read: 'Trams stop here by request'.

26

The No.26 tram passed two fine public facilities as it travelled along Grove Lane. These public baths, built in 1907, were a boon to swimmers – and bathers who had no bath at home. First and second class swimming pools, Turkish and private baths were available. The swimming baths were much used by local schools.

Sunday 18 September 1938. I went to Grove Lane Baths in the morning...Saw Margaret there. Looks a treat in a bathing costume. Oh! Boy!

Just beyond the baths appeared a main entrance to one of the city's most prestigious parks: Victoria Park, Handsworth, opened in 1887. For years it was the established venue for Boy Scouts' rallies, galas, flower and dog shows. Bowls, tennis, cricket and football could all be played there. The park pool was also a popular feature.

Monday 19 February 1940. Walked back through Handsworth Park. Boathouse roof down. Pool still frozen. Tons of snow about.

Wednesday 3 April 1940. First time I have managed a skiff out. Managed quite well, but you certainly have to be careful and sit tight.

A smaller park gate opens directly ahead of the lady, right. On most days of my secondary school attendance (1934-1939) and before evacuation took me to Stroud, I walked through that park entrance to and from school, including Saturday mornings. The road to the left of the bowler-hatted man is Douglas Road.

The driver of the motorcycle and sidecar, although leaning as if to hear what his passenger has to say, is still taking care to keep his wheels out of the tramlines. The tram has just passed one end of Holly Road. The two side roads visible are probably Chantry Road, left, and Leyton Road, right.

Handsworth Grammar School for Boys, left, was founded by the Bridge Trust in 1862. The four boys could be from the school having just left, perhaps, what was regarded as the school tuck shop. *Passing Show* featuring 'Plane Tales' was a colourful weekly magazine, while 'Slavery in our Cinemas', published in the magazine *Answers*, might be about the low pay of cinema staff?

At this crossroads Grove Lane joins Soho Road. The road opposite Grove Lane is Nineveh Road. On the corner, right, stands a rather elegant and modern building, a branch of the Municipal Savings Bank. This Birmingham bank was founded in 1916, the first of its kind in the country, an illustration of the aptness of the city's motto: Forward.

BIRMINGHAM CORPORATION
TRAMWAY & OMNIBUS DEPT.

Transport Facilities 1937

FORWARD

TRAMWAY SERVICES.

The No.6 tram is standing at its terminus, viewed from the Walsall or Aldridge Roads direction. The brick wall, left, forms part of the bridge over Perry Barr railway station. The two cyclists are giving the tramlines a wide berth. Near this spot, one of my brothers sustained a broken pelvis as a result of a traffic accident caused by his front bicycle wheel snagging in a tram line.

The date of this photograph could well be 25 May 1912. The open top deck and uncovered staircase support that view. On many Saturdays during the 1930s I collected a birdseed mixture from one of the shops, right, for an uncle – a nice little pocket money earner! The lady's bicycle has its chain encased, a sensible precaution with skirts so voluminous. Mrs Bloomer had not made her mark in Perry Barr!

Saturday 12 February 1938. Fetched Uncle George's birdseed. Played football in the afternoon.

This photograph was probably taken some twenty-five years later than the previous one. The Bundy time control clock on the pavement is 'new'. The relevant tram timetable for 1937 tells us that on weekdays the first No.6 of the day set off for Martineau Street at 0515 and the last tram home from town was 11.30pm.

A poignant message appears on the back of this card written on 19 August 1916. '...hope you will still keep mending. We have quite a lot of cripples knocking around here, I suppose we shall see more. Yes it's awful...' Almost certainly this is an allusion to the mind-stupefying casualties suffered on the Western Front during the First World War. The pub on the corner of Wellington Road, left, is the Crown and Cushion.

Old Crown and Cushion.

Although styled 'old', the Atkinson's house shown is the newest of the Crown and Cushion pubs that once stood either side of the Birchfield Road. From 1876 to 1897 an earlier Crown and Cushion on this site had served as Aston Villa's headquarters, its original ground being in Wellington Road. The lorry in that road is pointed towards Aston Lane, another route to Villa Park.

"SCOTT" SERIES, No. 1095

The steam tram is standing outside the original Perry Barr terminus, i.e. the Library. An undated but teasing message appears on the card's back. Phoebe tells Charlie: 'B'ham's motto is Forward (note tram). You have now got one in Manchester... Fancy the Villa losing on Sat. There must have been an accident somewhere but of course it pays the Villa to lose a game sometimes.' (!)

The lady in the light coloured hat is walking past the small but homely Birchfield Picture House, which opened in 1912. The 'Birchies' and the Odeon cinema (the first Odeon in Britain, 1930) were less than five minutes walk apart on Birchfield Road.

Tuesday 31 January 1939. Went with Margaret to see aforesaid pictures. Not particularly horrifying but thrilling all the same. Had a great time. (A spooky double bill, *Dracula* and *Frankenstein* at the Birchfield Picture House.)

Scribbled notes on this card's back suggest 1939 as the year of origin. The two schoolboys 'up top' are typical of the period. The tram, with driver Rowley and conductor Ernie Smith, has just passed the corner of The Broadway. Among the shops set back was my dad's favourite, which sold Firkin's pork pies. 'Despatch' (see front of tram) formed part of news vendors' bellowing cries of 'Spatchermail' as they sold copies of Birmingham's two evening papers.

From the Odeon citywards, to the junction with Trinity Road, left, and Heathfield Road, right, Birchfield Road was lined on both sides with fine large houses, screened by trees and laurel bushes aplenty. A corner of land by Heathfield Road was set aside for allotments. On the card's back a 'secret' message, arranging a date, can be read in a mirror.

The entrance to Trinity Road can now be seen, right. Trinity Road led and still leads to an arena of lay 'worship': Villa Park. An estimate of the combined length of the three ladders suggests that they may have been used for tramway pole maintenance work.

New Inn Road made a right angle turn from Birchfield Road to join the Heathfield Road. This photograph, dated 5 July 1949, was taken by W.A. Camwell, a noted photographer of Birmingham trams. The main advert is for BARBERS teas with 'Little Miss Barber' carrying the cup that cheers. The hard-wearing wavy 'blue brick' pavement, left, has not yet been replaced by concrete or asphalt blandness.

This is another Camwell card. It seems likely that the three people, left, have just got off the tram near Fentham Road, right. If so, did they drop their used tickets in the box provided at the other end of the tram platform? The houses in this stretch of Birchfield Road, though well built and spacious, are terraced and do not match the elegance of the property shown on the opposite page.

This photograph dates from August 1939. To the right of the tram runs Mansfield Road. At the corner 'Permanent Waving' on the ground floor with a café on the first, seem well matched. In front of the lorry a sharp hairpin bend left is the start of the Chain Walk which suffered heavy damage in the Autumn Blitz of 1940.

The steam tram has laboured up Birchfield Road before entering High Street, Aston, two of the six ways identified on the adjoining page. ' "Electric" trams have only been running since last Xmas anywhere in B'ham', writes the sender of the card postmarked 26 March 1907.

Six Ways, Aston, formed one of the busiest traffic hubs in the city. Tram routes leading to Perry Barr, Aston, Lozells and Witton crossed here. Of the six ways, only Alma Street lacked a tram route. Could that three-wheeled car heading towards Perry Barr be a full-of-character Morgan?

The Barton's Arms (facing), a fine Victorian building, has achieved something of icon status among Birmingham's pubs. Threatened with demolition, it has been restored with close attention to historic detail. The pub was popular not only with Aston residents but with audiences and performers at the Aston Hippodrome, right. Will Hay, listed on the music hall billboard, was a comedian who later starred in comedy films such as *Convict 99* and *Oh, Mr Porter!* The 'Aston Hipp' (now demolished) enjoyed a somewhat raffish reputation but was well patronised. The domed building on the left is the Globe Electric Palace, an early picture house opened in 1913. Cinemas like the Globe, situated in down-at-heel districts, were often known as 'flea-pits', more a term of affection than condemnation.

Well before the Second World War, it had been widely acknowledged that the Newtown area, with its back-to-back and tunnel-back housing, was badly in need of redevelopment. The depot towards which this tram is travelling is most probably the Miller Street depot off New Town Row.

This tram has stopped in Lancaster Street just short of a major tramway junction. The blank end wall of a factory building, left, carries an advert for 'Perry Pens'. Among Birmingham's so-called 1,001 trades, the manufacture of steel pen nibs occupied an important place.

This photograph has been taken from the tower of the new (1930s) central fire station. The tall brick tower, in Corporation Street, is part of Central Hall, 'HQ' of Birmingham's Methodists which served lay as well as religious purposes. The tram is pointing towards Steelhouse Lane, right, and Aston Street, left.

> *Wednesday 23 November 1938. Speech Day...Central Hall...I took tickets at top of stairs.*
> (Part of a prefect's duties!)

With luck, some No.6 passengers may well have seen a turnout like this.

Taking a course roughly parallel with Corporation Street, the No.6 tram would complete its journey at the city terminus in Martineau Street. The apex of the triangular building, left, carries some intriguing signs, e.g. 'Single Pairs'. Ahead, in Corporation Street, is the Cobden Hotel. Immediately to the right of the horse and cart is one entrance to Union Passage. The corner shop housed a firm noted for duplicating documents, namely Roneo Ltd.

Those were the days! A luncheon room sported table cloths, a café did not. This card was published when the postage stamp required cost a mere half-penny.

Not just some No.6 passengers but Brummies from all corners of the city would flock to their beloved Bull Ring. The right to hold markets on what had been a village green had existed for more than 800 years. Barrows and stalls piled high with fruit, vegetables, flowers; soapbox orators and entertainers shouting the odds; a large indoor market and jostling, good-natured crowds all combined to create a highly colourful and happy, rather than humdrum, atmosphere of buying and selling. The church of St Martin's seemed to look on benignly. In the foreground, right, a poster for the Grand Theatre gives Mrs Lily Langtry, the 'Jersey Lily', top billing.

Monday 11 April 1938. Elijah presented by School Choir at St Martin's Church, Bull Ring. Singing O.K. Monday 3 April 1939. School Choral Society's presentation of St Matthew's Passion...came out before it finished so that I could see Margaret. (Core material here for several sermons!)

Starting at Martineau Street the services 3 and 3X run to Witton, the 3 via Six Ways, Aston, and the 3X via Aston Cross. Various other northerly tram services ran along Aston Street, specifically the 2, 78 and 79. In the distance can be seen a number of trams at the busy intersection of Lancaster Place. The top of the tower, right, is that of the 1930s central fire station.

This postcard was posted in Guernsey in 1907. The horse bus is moving across from Park Road to Lichfield Road. The clock tower replaced Aston's Old Cross which once marked the entrance to the private estates of a notable family whose history was closely linked to that of Aston Hall, long a visitor attraction.

Mention Aston Cross to some elderly Brummies and they may well refer to the fragrances of yesteryear emanating from the nearby HP Sauce factory and from Ansells Brewery. The Midland Vinegar Co. started to produce vinegar in 1897 and the famous sauce in 1905.

This card provides a closer view of a modernised Ansells. From small beginnings in 1881, Ansells had grown by 1890 to become one of five major brewers in the Birmingham area, the other four being Holt Brewery, Mitchell, Davenport and Atkinsons. The No.2 tram is making for Erdington while the 78 is heading for town from Short Heath.

Aston Library, right, is standing on the corner of Albert Road just a short distance from Six Ways, Aston. The sign, above the boy, reads: 'Cars stop here by request.' Walking to the east down Albert Road would bring the walker to Aston Grammar School, a school of the King Edward's Foundation.

A No.3 tram is at its Witton terminus. The shops with the awnings bear the legend 'Birmingham Co-operative Society'. Rarely can a traffic island be associated with romance, but...
   Friday 28 October 1938...she says meet me at half-past six at island Witton. Yippee!
The edge of the island can just be seen near the third awning.

Sometimes all the fun of the fair was to be had, especially in October at the Serpentine Ground, Witton, where the annual Onion Fair was held.

Saturday 29 October 1938. Went to fair at night with Margaret. Had a great time. You bet. Held her hand a lot of times. Went on Wheel, Waltzer (upset her), Dodgems 2, Over the Sticks, Ghost Train, Wall of Death, Boxing.

Here is revealed the mundane but essential reality of the tram depot at Witton. By regularly servicing trams and providing extra cars, the unpublicised depot workers were of great but largely unrecognised help to the fair goer and football fan, bent on pleasure.

Roughly every other Saturday between September and April, thousands of football fans would make Witton their Mecca in order to cheer on Aston Villa. Many 'special' trams would be laid on, as shown here in Trinity Road. Opposite this line of trams runs one of the boundaries of Aston Park.

> *Saturday 26 August 1939. Went to Villa match. They beat Middlesborough 2-0. Very good game. Nobody suffering from crisitis. First thing men at the match did when they bought evening papers was to look at racing results on the back page. Typical illustration of man in street's unconcern.*

War was declared on 3 September 1939. ('Crisitis' – an invented word.)

Many of the above would have played in the reported game. Frankie Broome (extreme left, front row) was the one to watch, a quicksilver forward.

Three
North-Eastern Routes

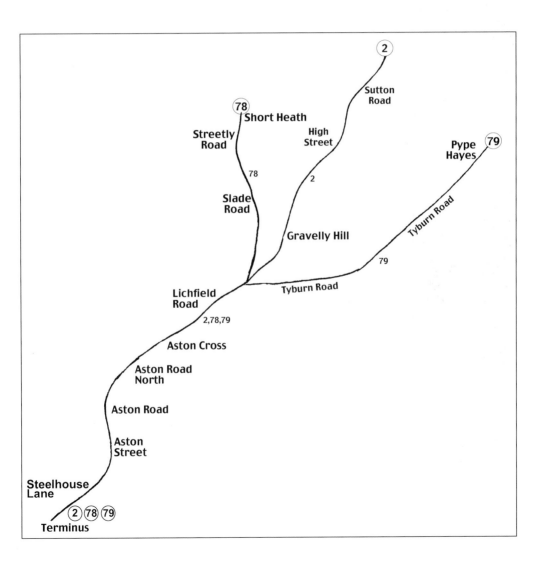

The longest tram route running roughly north was that of the No.2 service from Steelhouse Lane to the city boundary just beyond Chester Road, a distance of some five miles. Along part of the same route ran the No.5 via the Lozells, Lichfield Road to Gravelly Hill, Erdington. The 78 and 79 services took the same route as the No.2 as far as Gravelly Hill where the 78 branched left to Stockland Green and Short Heath and the 79 right, along the Tyburn Road to Chester Road, near Pype Hayes Park.

The terminus signboard makes very plain the 78's destinations. This stop stands outside the dignified and stately columned Wesleyan & General Insurance building. A little further on, the MON forms part of the GAUMONT PALACE cinema sign. It is claimed by some that this cinema was Birmingham's favourite. Opening with *Raffles* in 1931 and starring Ronald Colman, the British heart-throb actor, the cinema remained viable for the next fifty years.

For a time, this was Birmingham's finest hospital, just a short distance from the tram terminus on the previous page. Opened in 1897 by Princess Christian, daughter of Queen Victoria, the hospital contained 340 beds. All too soon its cheery red bricks became soot-begrimed in the city's industrial atmosphere.

A few yards more and the Steelhouse Lane tram passengers would have gained this view of the new fire station at Lancaster Place. The station is bounded to the left by Corporation Street and to the right by Aston Road. This fire station was well placed to tackle fires in the city centre during Birmingham's blitz of 1940-1941.

After travelling along Aston Road, trams would pass Aston Cross (see page 44) and the massive Dunlop, later Hercules, bicycle works. Then followed Lichfield Road, a busy main thoroughfare through this highly industrialised suburb of which the chimney stacks were symbolic. The bridge ahead of the tram is that of Aston railway station.

Only inches to spare! This bridge replaced an older one, the original hoisting being featured on a number of postcards claiming that: 'this Bridge, weighing 300 tons, was placed in position in 15½ minutes. A Great Engineering Feat', carried out on Sunday 25 March 1906. The famous 'Good Honest Beer' slogan refers, of course, to Mitchells and Butlers brews.

The photograph, taken in 1952, shows the 78 car setting down passengers at Gravelly Hill before turning into Slade Road and onwards to Short Heath. The lorry, right, appears to be turning into Tyburn Road. The No.2 will climb Gravelly Hill on its route to Erdington 'village'. This tramway crossing has been absorbed by the notorious 'Spaghetti' motorway junction.

The tram, in Slade Lane, appears to be slowed down to the horse and cart pace set by the 'vehicle' in front. On this poorly tinted card, signposts, immediately above WINES, point left to the city centre and right to Sutton Coldfield. Atkinson's Aston Ales became part of the M&B empire in 1959.

This tram is bowling along in leafy suburbia in the direction of Stockland Green. That a piano firm should be advertising on the front of the tram suggests that the days of the 'joanna' in the parlour, symbolising lower middle class respectability, are not yet gone. The tall fence and hedge, left, could be one of the boundaries of Highcroft Hall, a mental hospital.

On the cart, left, milk churns are discernible. The long building in the background is the Stockland Green Hotel, a modern M&B house with parking space. The single-decker outer circle bus is making for Reservoir Road which leads to Six Ways, Erdington. The postmark on the card, though blurred, looks like 1926, the year when the outer circle bus service was inaugurated. In the same year the tram terminus was extended on reserved track to Short Heath.

This first tram made its inaugural journey northwards along Sutton Road to Birmingham's boundary with Sutton near Harman Road. Appropriately the driver was William Lee, the chairman of the Tramways Committee in Birmingham and a member of Erdington UDC.

'Archer's Supply Stores', left, is on the corner of Reservoir Road. People at the barrier are waiting for a tram to come down High Street to take them to Gravelly Hill or beyond in the direction of the city centre. The traffic island was one of the first to be installed in England in 1926. The church stands on the corner of Wood End Road.

Trams had to operate on a single track through this narrow section of the village. The tram is close by the double track section. The Erdington Picture House was built in 1913. Although small, this cinema was popular and boasted an orchestra in silent film days. It closed in 1956.

This scene gives a clearer view of the single track and is indicative of the original village nature of Erdington, which did not become part of Birmingham until 1911. The second awning, left, seems to be emblazoned with FRED KINGS NATURALIST, presumably a herbalist. The card was posted in 1924.

This small and formal triangular flowerbed, at the northern end of High Street, can be regarded as a memorial to the demise of a pukka village green. The shop on the corner, right, is Shufflebothams Stores. The shop with the awning appears to be a 'First class meat purveyor' while next door is Leah Taylor's, seemingly a ladies' dress shop.

As the result of traffic congestion, in which a narrow high street played a key part, a by-pass was built and completed in 1938. On Sutton New Road, double tram tracks were provided along a central reservation. This work necessitated the demolition of some old property.

THE TRAFFIC CONTROL ISLAND. SUTTON & CHESTER RD'S. ERDINGTON

Rapidly increasing traffic brought increased traffic controls and street furniture. Traffic islands ceased to be a novelty. The signs pointing left indicate Aldridge, Walsall and Chester, some seventy plus miles distant on the A452. 'Yenton' of the Yenton Garage, right, is held by some to be a possible corruption of 'Yerdington' which has long been Erdington.

TRAM TERMINUS. ERDINGTON & YENTON HOTEL

This card, posted in 1932, not only shows the tram terminus, but the modern pub, left of the tram, called Yenton, like the garage above. An old rhyme runs:

Sutton for mutton / Tamworth for beef / Yenton for a pretty girl / …

The last line has been omitted for being highly uncomplimentary to Brummies!

At Gravelly Hill (see page 53) the 79 tram turned right into Tyburn Road to continue as far as Pype Hayes Park. The development of this section of the route was prompted by the move of Dunlop in 1916 from Aston to a semi-rural site close by Birmingham Racecourse. This route was one of the last three to be closed, the others being the 2 and 78.

At the top of this aerial photograph can be seen, left, some of the bends of Birmingham Racecourse. In between the two sites of work and leisure run a railway line and the River Tame. John Dunlop (1840-1921), an Irish veterinary surgeon, can hardly have envisaged that his successful experiments with the pneumatic tyre would develop into a massive business empire affecting many people's lives.

This photograph was taken on 9 May 1953, a few short weeks before the last day of the tram service to Fort Dunlop.

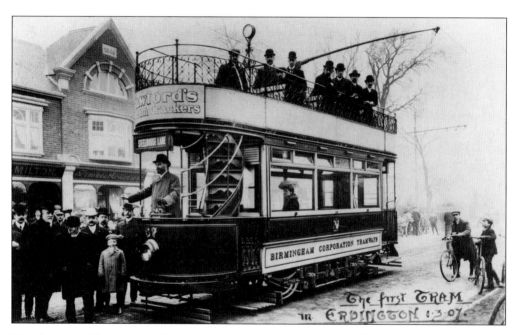

Worth a second look? A celebration to contrast new with ebbing life. The driver is Mr William Lee, already mentioned on page 55, who won the day against those who had claimed that 'tramcars would endanger the lives of people – particularly children – when crossing the roads, frighten horses and, by causing residences to be overlooked from the trams, to reduce their value. It was also said that the rural aspect of the district would be ruined.'

Four
Eastern Routes

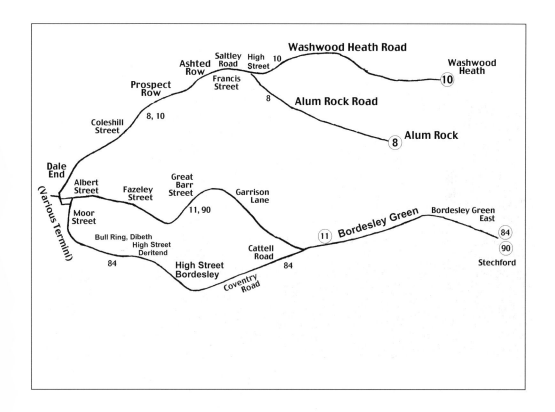

Public transport services to Nechells experienced a somewhat chequered history. After horse and steam trams, the No.7 electric tram route which ran along Great Lister Street to Nechells ceased in 1922, to be replaced by trolleybuses which themselves stopped running in 1940.

While overhead electric wiring remains in place, tramlines have been removed. This was carried out in 1922 when a temporary bus service was provided before the introduction of trolleybuses on this route.

On the back of this card Ada writes to her mother in Barnsley that 'we live opposite where the car is stopped.' Running due east, Washwood Heath Road formed the last stretch of the No.10 route and passed Ward End Park before reaching its terminus.

Information on this card's back states: 'Metropolitan Works Sports at Washwood Heath', 12 May 1928. The six finalists lining up for the Midland quarter mile championship include P. Jeavons, A.W. Green, J.H.A. Hawkins and H. Houghton of the internationally renowned club of Birchfield Harriers, S. Spencer from Sutton Harriers and W.H. Spencer of Leicester. The leaping golden stag of the Birchfield Harriers can plainly be seen on the black vest of the second from right runner. NB – no staggered start!

"Fox and Goose" and Beaufort Cinema.

The Fox and Goose, left, on the corner with Bromford Lane, constituted a modernised rebuilding of a much earlier pub of the same name. The mock Tudor Beaufort, right, behind the trees, was opened in 1929 and improved internally in 1937 to hold 1,500 cinema-goers. It closed in 1978.

Uncrowded roads, a spacious layout of buildings – when motoring was fun! On the traffic island the signposts, left, are headed: Warwick, Stratford, Alcester, Stechford, Acocks Green, and, right: Sutton, Lichfield, Erdington. Besides the Fox and Goose pub, right, stands a tram barely distinguishable from its background of trees.

'Transport Facilities 1937' an official Birmingham Corporation timetable, see page 31, lists two tram routes where suburban termini are identified by a pub. One is New Inns, Handsworth (rush periods only) the No.28 service, and the 10, Fox and Goose, Washwood Heath. Brewery 'patronage' seems fairly divided, the New Inns being an M&B house with the Fox and Goose belonging to Ansells. The Fox and Goose terminus was established in 1913.

Grannie writes on the back of this card (posted in 1919): '...this is where I go shopping sometimes.' Did her shopping list include 'double collars'? Such collars appear to be among the merchandise advertised, left, at first floor level. St Julien tobacco is advertised across the street at the same height.

"The Pelham," Alum Rock.

Left: 'The Pelham' is a reference to the Pelham Arms, an M&B house in Pelham Road, just beyond the terminus for the No.8 service to Alum Rock. The card, seemingly one of a series, was published for Woods, 'Stationers…884 Alum Rock Road'. On its fender the tram exhorts people to 'Cross Crossings Cautiously'. Alliteration does help the memory! It is sometimes forgotten that, except on reservations or purpose built islands, trams, unlike buses, could not draw to a kerbside. The area between pavement and tram platform steps could indeed be hazardous.

The tram shown bears the sign 'Small Heath Park to Station Street', that street being close to the main line railway station of New Street. Small Heath Park was a gift (1876) from Miss Louisa Anne Ryland, a noted Birmingham philanthropist. (See also page 78.) The building, right, with arched windows, advertises 'Walker's Burton Ales' while next door 'Lilly's' appears to be a snappy gents' outfitters.

Steam trams that ran along Coventry Road were replaced by electric cars in 1905. Small Heath was a highly industrialised suburb, being home to major manufacturing companies such as Wolseley and BSA. The area was also home to Birmingham City FC at St Andrew's. Small Heath Park (see previous page) opened in 1879.

Red Hill lay roughly halfway between the above park and South Yardley. The tramway was not extended along the Coventry Road to Sheldon as might have been expected, but replaced by trolleybuses in 1934, service 93 to Yardley and 94 to the Coventry Road city boundary.

67

This scene is thought to date from 1912, the route having been opened in 1906 starting from Albert Street. From 1915 this service became No.11. The card's sender lived in Churchill Road, Bordesley Green. From a similar postcard J.R. Burn is clearly a tobacconist.

This, clearly, is a tram for all seasons. According to information on the back, the photograph was taken at Stechford. It is as well to remember that tram photographers naturally showed a partiality for clicking their shutters on fine rather than foul weather days. But trams, and their crews, had to venture out in all weathers.

Again according to information on the back, this photograph was taken on 13 July 1938. There is pleasing symmetry about the line of six trams, poles all pointing the same way, three from the 84 service and three from the 90, arranged one by one alternately, with an 84 seemingly heading the line travelling back to town.

Tram routes to the south-eastern suburbs of Acocks Green and Hall Green were relatively short-lived. By 1937 the sector of the city between Yardley and Warstock/Yardley Wood was served entirely by buses and trolleybuses. In earlier years trams had run along the Stratford Road through Sparkbrook and Sparkhill.

On the back of this card someone has dated the scene as being from 1907 and the route being followed as Sparkbrook to Washwood Heath. The Gaiety Theatre, advertised on the tram, was a music hall located in Coleshill Street (in town) which became a cinema in 1920.

Some of the passengers on these early trams may well have alighted near Walford Road. During roughly 1906-1912 roller skating was all the rage in Britain. At least four rinks were opened in Birmingham of which the above was one. A small orchestra provided music, café refreshments and the rink itself many opportunities for courtship preliminaries.

Stratford Road, Sparkhill.

Some interesting shop window displays feature on this section of the tram route. Amongst other goods, the library seems to have what look like postcards for sale. Wharams re-cover and repair, as well as sell, umbrellas. The shop next door seems to be Paynes, and could be a branch of a well known shoe repair firm of that name. The chemist has hung out a discreet sign for Iron Jelloids – 'the greatest of all tonics', as some will recall.

Tram Terminus.
Acocks Green

With the arrival, in 1852, of the railway, the rural Acocks Green community began to expand. A tram route, 44, from the city began in 1916 and was subsequently extended along Warwick Road to the junction with Westley Road in 1922. But trams had to yield to buses in January 1937. The traffic island is an enlarged one to accommodate the extended route.

This route 18 tram is ascending a hilly section of Stratford Road in the area known as Springfield. As a facetious schoolboy, the 'Marsh's Sausages' advertisement appealed to me greatly. The pig is harnessed to a trolley laden with large sausages, the rather cruel (for today) caption reading: 'Drawing his own conclusion.'

Hall Green is another rural area which became a residential suburb. This photograph captures something of that leafy, comfortable character. Trams first reached Hall Green in 1914 and eventually continued to the city boundary in 1928. But all tram services along the Stratford Road ceased in 1937.

This card was posted in 1933 and clearly shows the reserved track for trams, a particular feature of the route to Hall Green. In typical motherly fashion the lady seems to be making sure that her son's hair is tidy before the awaited tram is boarded.

Dating from 1913, Hall Green Parade constituted a row of good shops, including a chemist and a stationer, with trams running close by. From being a quiet rural area, Hall Green became a much sought after residential suburb with good quality housing set in pleasing surroundings.

Some Facts and Figures

1903   Preparations for expansion of tramway system exemplified by creation of a new municipal office, that of Tramway Manager. Mr Alfred Baker, manager of London County Council Tramways appointed. Annual salary £1,300 rising to £1,500.

1907   Adoption of overhead electric wiring system.

1909   '...considerable concession to the motormen and conductors,' their working hours being reduced from sixty to fifty-four per week.

1911   All city tramlines owned and managed by Corporation. Tram numbers increased from 300 to 465.

1914-1918   First World War. 1,792 tramways employees served in the Forces, of whom 210 were killed. Women were recruited to the tramways to replace men, many serving as conductresses. By 1917 some 1,200 women were on the payroll.

1918-1935   A period of steady and continuing expansion of both tram and bus services.

1930   Introduction of cheaper fares on trams and buses, known as Workmen's Returns, and related to journeys before 9.00 a.m. with no time restriction for return journeys. Maximum return fare: 5 pence.

1935   Town planning methods and new housing estates exerted a 'potent influence' on the municipal transport system. By this time some 42,000 council houses had been built, affecting approximately 180,000 people, a major population re-distribution. Number of trams: 758, motor buses: 554, trolley buses: 66, and total staff around 6,800.

1939-1945   Second World War. Over 1,100 employees, including many reservists, were called up at the outbreak of war and 2,129 eventually experienced war service. Women were again recruited to serve as replacements, many becoming 'clippies'. Birmingham experienced seventy-seven air raids, the six heaviest occurring between 26/27 August 1940 and 9/10 April 1941 accounting for some 4,500 deaths. Forty-one trams and twenty motor buses were destroyed and around 1,500 vehicles damaged.

1946-1953   Decline and demise.

There are many ways in which statistics may be used to illustrate the dimensions of the Corporation's tramways service, but perhaps the best method for present purposes is to use the measure of Passengers Carried. Corresponding figures for motor buses (petrol and diesel) are also given to demonstrate the wax and wane of the two main transport services.

Passengers Carried

Financial Year	Trams	Buses
1907-1908	75,601,195	
1914-1915	149,443,199	
1927-1928	254,125,984	62,353,311
Figure stayed above 200 million until:		
1934-1935	191,349,666	154,007,505
1935-1936	191,318,526	167,557,566
1936-1937	186,576,388	190,464,952
1937-1938	174,023,634	225,063,912
1949-1950	102,453,436	417,495,056

Five
Southern and South-Western Routes

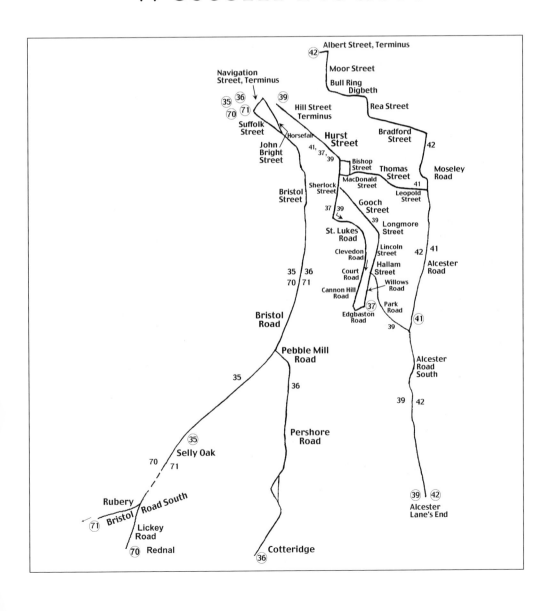

By a somewhat convoluted route the 37 service made its way from Navigation Street to Cannon Hill. The start of its journey through a built-up inner city area, as shown in these two cards, contrasts strongly with its destination of Cannon Hill with its fine trees, park and sports fields.

Here the trams are in Gooch Street looking towards the city centre. Highgate Street is slanting away to the right. Both photographs were apparently taken on 27 June 1949. Above the corner grocers, Chadwicks, little Miss Barber is still delivering the cup that cheers and a 'Benedict Peas' advert appears on the striped awning.

From information on this card's back, 'this route re-started but rush hours only + Saturday aft & Sunday.' This is a wartime photograph dated 11 June 1941; note the lower part of the terminus clock is painted white, no doubt to ease the stumbling about that inevitably occurred in the blackout. The standards and kerbstones have been similarly treated.

During the period under review (1874-1953) few would deny that for elegance and wealth, as represented by fine residential property, Moseley and Edgbaston were Birmingham's two grandest suburbs. The destination of the above tram is Cannon Hill Park. Service 37 from Navigation Street was single track and necessitated a loop along Cannon Hill Road and Willows Road near the Warwickshire County Cricket Ground.

In 1873 Miss Louisa Anne Ryland (see also page 66) donated land to the city to provide recreation and relaxation for Birmingham people. Some enthusiasts hoped that the Main Drive might come to rival Rotten Row in London. It was not to be, but tennis in the park became popular as can be seen, right, as did the fine boating pool and immaculate formal gardens.

This county eleven, photographed at the county ground (c.1895) close by Cannon Hill Park, contains two men who played for England. A.A. Lilley made thirty-five appearances as wicketkeeper between 1896 and 1909. W.G. Quaife, batsman, made his debut for the national side in 1899 and finished his appearances with four runs in 1902.

Above & below: In terms of photographers' viewpoints, these cards are closely comparable. Steam trams had begun running to Moseley in 1884. The message on the lower card was written in 1916. So, during a span of twenty to thirty years, when a major change had occurred in public transport, the outward appearance of the buildings shown remained much the same. A spot-the-difference yields little. Some tidying up has taken place; the pavement displays of goods for sale on the earlier postcard have disappeared, possibly to raise the tone of the village to that of its well-to-do residential surroundings?

Use of a magnifying glass establishes that the tram's route is King's Heath (via) Bradford Street which runs from Digbeth to Camp Hill. This 42 service set out from Albert Street, near Dale End. Reading from the left, the third awning displays the intriguing words: 'Publicans in the Trade Supplied.'

The message on this card begins: 'Sorry you all had to get up for German visitors…' As it is addressed to London and posted on 6 September 1917, this may well be a typically British way of referring to an air raid on the capital.

In 1937 Navigation Street formed the departure point for no less that seven tram services (including one rush period service) that headed roughly south-west. After an eight mile journey to Rednal, much of it along the A38, the gateway to the Lickey Hills was reached. The 35 travelled to Selly Oak, being the rush period service mentioned above. Finlays provided a number of tobacco product kiosks. The scene dates from 1952.

The top-hatted driver of this well-laden Hansom cab is driving his vehicle towards the city, perhaps carrying his fare to New Street Station. Bristol Street preceded Bristol Road, which was followed by Bristol Road South and Lickey Road. Hansom cabs are named after their inventor, Joseph Hansom, but are better remembered for their association with Sherlock Holmes' adventures.

It is open to discussion whether this driver, fashionably attired in long coat, cap and driving gloves, has wandered into the tramlines or chosen to drive in them. The card was posted in 1911 and gives a good impression of the generous width of the road and pavements.

Again the spacious nature of roads and pavements can be judged, by the size of the tram in relation to its setting. The appreciable distances between solid and imposing gateposts and the privacy of their owners ensured by the screening trees are indicative of the well-heeled status of Edgbaston.

The University, Birmingham

Although Birmingham University began life as Mason's College in the city centre, it was on the Bristol Road that the redbrick campus was developed. King Edward VII and Queen Alexandra made the formal opening in 1909. The clock tower was dubbed 'Joe' in honour of Sir Joseph Chamberlain, the first University Chancellor and a major driving force behind many city improvement schemes.

A photograph taken in 1952 of trams passing under a railway bridge close to Selly Oak railway station. 'Joe' can just be seen in the hazy distance. A couple of years earlier, as an ex-serviceman undergraduate at the Arts Faculty at Edmund Street, I travelled on Bristol Road trams to play in only semi-serious games of hockey on the university's sports field.

MOTOR TERMINUS SELLY OAK.

At one time, Selly Oak was as far as trams ran. Travellers to the Lickeys would then need to catch the open top bus to Rednal. The Plough and Harrow, left, selling Holts Ales, stands on the corner of Chapel Lane. The Holt Brewery became part of Ansells in 1934. The bus service mentioned, starting in 1913, was provided by Birmingham Corporation.

THE CROSS ROAD'S, BRISTOL RD, SELLY OAK

This crossroads was one of the city's busiest traffic junctions. Left is Oak Tree Lane along which the outer circle bus carried passengers to Cadbury's, Bournville and Stirchley. To the right is Harborne Lane and the No.11 bus route through Harborne to Bearwood. The tram, a blurred image, is making for Northfield.

The Woodlands, Bristol Road South, Northfield.

The Woodlands is the fine white house, set in extensive grounds. Once the home of a member of the Cadbury family, it was given away by him to become the Royal Cripples Hospital, renamed the Royal Orthopaedic Hospital. On long stretches of the Bristol Road, the tram tracks to Rednal and Rubery were carried on central reservations completed in the 1920s.

Trams on the A38 and approaching Northfield 'village' would pass this M&B pub situated between Whitehill Lane and Bell Lane. Presumably, putting a thatched roof on a self-evidently new pub was, at the time, a marketing experiment. This card was published by the brewery.

The Village, Bristol Road South, Northfield.

Pigeon House Hill, Northfield.

330-17.

A close scrutiny of this card clearly reveals throngs of day-trippers making their ways, almost in crocodile fashion, up and down Bilberry Hill. On the road below, more trippers are joining the queue. A visit to the popular Bilberry Tea-Rooms brought extra enjoyment. For many people in the days when men wore the flat caps as shown, days out were few and far between. Opportunities abounded for 'a jolly good ramble', 'a spot of courting' or simply to be alone or with a few friends to enjoy Nature. From hills scaled by stepped slopes, see left, good views could be had and, on grassy slopes, impromptu games of cricket and football could be played. With the passing of time and a much wider range of leisure activities, the appeal of this area has changed. Fairly recent publicity states: 'Lickey Hills Country Park. Over 500 acres of deciduous and coniferous woodland, marshy areas and heathland, with a rich variety of wildlife.'

Opposite, above: Not until 1911 was Northfield incorporated from Worcestershire into Birmingham. Because of village topography, it was not feasible to extend the central reservation for trams through the main shopping street. To the left of the tram Bell Hill makes a steep descent before rising to a hillside where extensive housing developments have been built.

Opposite, below: Not far to the Lickeys now! Trams would make good speed down this hill to pass the massive Austin Longbridge works, the 70 service continuing up Lickey Road to the terminus at Rednal, 'gateway' to the Lickey Hills. These offered, especially for Brummies of the 1920s and '30s, a fine day out in really fresh air and attractive countryside. The No.71 tram curved away right at Longbridge, on Bristol Road South to Rubery.

    Saturday 14 September 1940. Set back at 8 Rednal. Warnings went had to alight. Walked Bristol Rd. Miles. Bus 11. Home 1/4 10.

The 'good old outer circle bus' was caught at Selly Oak.

As intimated earlier, some tram services which used the Bristol Road branched away from that road. The tram shown is almost certainly a 36 – Navigation Street to Cotteridge. This stretch of central reservation track is in Pebble Mill Road where BBC radio and television studios are now to be found. Laid in 1919, the reserved track was the first in the city but many more and lengthier stretches were to be built in the next few years.

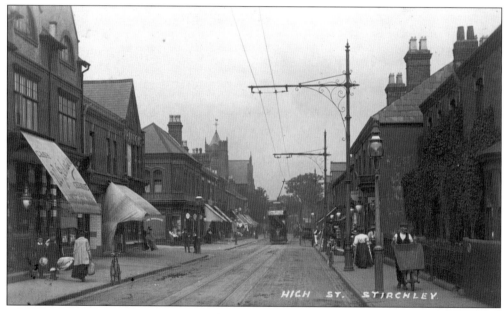

Here is another illustration of a village high street being brought within the reach of a tram service. Stirchley is just a few stops short of Cotteridge, a tram destination since 1904. To the left of the tram runs Mary Vale Road, affording an easy walk to work for some tram travellers employed by Cadbury's in Bournville Lane.

Six

Western and North-Western Routes

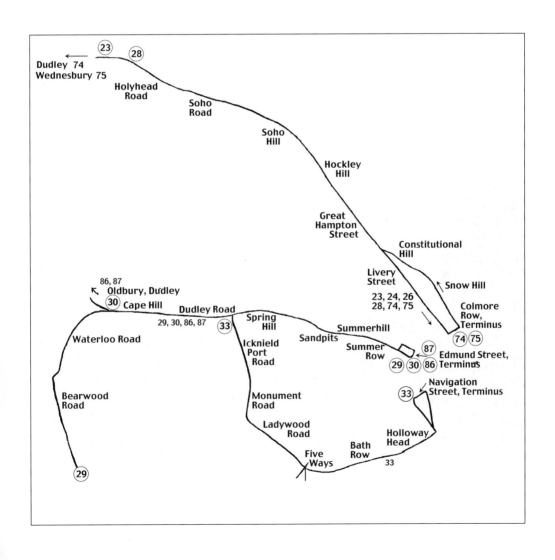

Seven trams, all in Navigation Street, can be spotted on this view against the backdrop of the massive railway station. Dating back to the 1850s, New Street station had been doubled in size in 1880 to straddle, as here, Queens Drive. The spire of St Martin's church in the Bull Ring can be seen in line with that Drive.

> *Friday 16 February 1940. Went home…Snowing when we arrived at New Street. Atrocious weather. Snow in large mounds down either side of the road. Good to see Mom and Dad again.*

(A short break at home. School was evacuated to Stroud.)

The No.33 passed along Islington Row on its way to and from Ladywood, its terminus being near Summerfield Park. The dignified, column-fronted building, right, is a branch of Lloyds Bank. The card, used for birthday greetings to 'Dad' was posted in June 1920.

Five Ways once marked the boundary between Edgbaston and Birmingham. To the left is Broad Street and to the right lies Calthorpe Road. The standing statue is of Joseph Sturge (1794-1859) merchant and Quaker philanthropist, pro-adult suffrage Radical and anti-slavery campaigner. The tram is climbing out of Islington Row.

A proud Brummie writes: 'Dear David, this is only one of our parks…and only about 10 minutes walk' (presumably from home). Having a green oasis, complete with bandstand would mean a great deal to many people living in the densely crowded areas of Winson Green and Ladywood. One of the park's boundaries was formed by Dudley Road. Another was near the 33's terminus.

Dudley Road formed an important section of various tram routes leading to the Black Country. Here, tram passengers visiting sick relatives in hospital could be set down. Dudley Road Hospital has undergone changes that closely reflect what has happened in society. From Victorian workhouse, the buildings became an infirmary, smallpox hospital, scarlet fever hospital and latterly a vastly improved general hospital.

Having passed near the hospital, trams would continue past the entrance to Winson Green Road, left on the card. Along that road and on the corner of Lodge Road, stood Winson Green Prison.

'Blondes for Danger' is a debatable if enticing issue, but the Grove Picture House, in Dudley Road, close to the boundary with Smethwick, was unquestionably a modern cinema, being opened in 1932. The photograph was taken on 30 August 1939 near the Grove Lane, Smethwick crossover, a few days before the outbreak of the Second World War.

The terminus of the No.30 service from Edmund Street 'rush periods only' was Cape Hill, close to the massive M&B brewery. This coloured card is one of a number published by the company to celebrate its Golden Jubilee in 1929. The artist's rather impressionistic drawing shows two trams on Cape Hill.

After Cape Hill, service 29 would fork left down Waterloo Road then Bearwood Road to finish its journey near Hagley Road. Opposite Three Shires Oak Road is Sandon Road, a good shopping area. The corner shop, left, is Fosters', possibly a branch of the well-known multiple, men's clothing firm.

At the western end of Cape Hill, services 86, Edmund Street to Oldbury, and 87, Edmund Street to Dudley, turned right at Dudley Road where an old toll house once stood, to make their way through Smethwick, along High Street. The dignified building next to the awning is a branch of the Midland Bank. A branch of Lloyds Bank stands on the opposite turreted corner.

Of the various services that travelled west from the city centre, four made their way along
Holyhead Road, an extension of Soho Road. Two, the 23 and 28, stopped just short of or at the
city boundary. Two others, the 74 and 75 carried on to Dudley and Wednesbury respectively.
    Monday 10 April 1939 (Easter Monday). Went to Aunt Molls. (Netherton, near
    Dudley.) *Buses make journey much quicker.* On the other hand: *Saturday 6 August
    1938. Dame tried to get off with me on tram.* No doubt wishful thinking on my part,
    being but fifteen and impressionable. (Another visit to Black Country relatives.)
    *Friday 25 October 1940. Stap me! Knocked an old chap down in Holyhead Rd this
    morning.* (I was on a bicycle. No great harm done to either party – or to bike.)

This photograph was taken on 24 September 1938 outside the Hawthorns, West Bromwich
Albion's football ground. The two lines of trams are waiting for the game's final whistle to
blow. Left are the trams for some of the 'Baggies' Black Country supporters and, right, their
Brummagem fans – and possibly some supporters of the visiting team. Conductors can be
identified by the bell punches around their necks.
    *Saturday 23 September 1939. Walked to the Hawthorns in the afternoon and watched the
    'Baggies' play the 'Wolves'. Quite a good game. Westcott a real live wire leader for the Wolves.
    Banged in 3 peach goals for them. Wolves won 5-3 after being two down at half-time.*

Having crossed the city boundary, trams would enter a high street resembling many others where erstwhile village centres had been linked together by tram or bus services. Only a few of the profusion of shop signs can be read and a magnifier is needed for 'Weldons Fashions' above the little girl's head.

This is a 75 tram to Wednesbury at the point where High Street joins Carters Green to be followed by Dudley Street and the generous, good-hearted world of Enoch and Eli, wherein exists an inexhaustible store of humorous Black Country stories and sayings. 'Ow many am ther on we?' conveys a little something of the dialect flavour.

Close to the 74's terminus was the entrance to the grounds containing the ruins of Dudley Castle. In the late 1930s a highly popular state-of-the-art zoo was built near the foot of the castle. Catch the tram and pay a visit! Imaginative use was made of old limestone pits which allowed far more space and fresh air for lions, for example, than was usual at that time.

Monday 25 March 1940 (Easter Monday). Wonderful pits for lions, tigers and bears. Sea-lions clever and amusing. The zoo is a very interesting and entertaining place.

This card has been included because of its tram connection, i.e. the three clocks. The lettering above the middle clock reads: 'Next Car Departs At'. Underneath each clock are three named destinations. I have only been able to decipher two of the three termini under the central clock, namely Netherton and Cradley. The clocks show that the three trams are to depart within five minutes of one another.

FIRST AND LAST CARS
ON ALL ROUTES TO AND FROM CITY.
(Bank Holidays excepted.)

To City. Weekdays First Cars a.m.	Last Cars p.m.	Sundays First Cars a.m.	Last Cars p.m.	Service No.		From City. Weekdays First Cars a.m.	Last Cars p.m.	Sundays First Cars a.m.	Last Cars p.m.
6-43	10-58	10-15	10-58	39	Alcester Lanes End and Hill St. (via Balsall Heath).	6-44	11-30	9-42	11-30
5-3	11-0	8-43	11-0	42	Alcester Lanes End and Albert St. (via Bradford Street)	5-37	11-30	9-13	11-30
—	—	10-20	11-0	51	Alcester Lanes End and Hill Street (via Leopold Street)	—	—	9-48	10-30
5-8	11-10	8-51	11-10	8	Alum Rock and Martineau St.	5-28	11-30	9-13	11-30
5-28	11-8	8-50	11-8	49	Balsall Heath and Hill Street	5-8	11-30	9-13	11-30
5-28	11-6	8-44	11-6	29	Bearwood and Edmund St.	5-35	11-30	9-8	11-30
4-58	11-12	9-57	11-12	11	Bordesley Green and Seymour Street (via Fazeley Street)	5-18	11-30	10-18	11-30
5-27	11-10	8-54	11-10	12	Bordesley Green and Albert Street (via Deritend)	5-48	11-30	9-13	11-30
4-43	11-8	8-48	11-8	46	British Oak, Stirchley and Navigation Street.	5-15	11-30	9-11	11-30
7-28	11-15	8-58	11-15	37	Cannon Hill and Navigation Street.	7-28	11-30	9-13	11-30
4-38	11-3	8-43	11-3	36	Cotteridge and Navigation St.	5-15	11-30	9-11	11-30
4-58	†10-28	9-15	10-36	74	Dudley and Colmore Row (via West Bromwich).	5-52	10-38	9-38	10-35
5-36	10-32	9-32	10-32	87	Dudley and Edmund Street (via Smethwick).	6-14	10-14	9-13	10-14
5-15	11-12	8-55	11-12	6	Perry Barr and Martineau St.	5-33	11-30	9-13	11-30
5-20	11-1	8-43	11-1	79	Pype Hayes and Steelhouse Lane.	5-18	11-30	9-13	11-30
5-30	10-40b	8-28	10-50	70	Rednal and Navigation Street.	5-18	11-30	9-12	11-30
5-40f	10-48	8-23	10-44	71	Rubery and Navigation Street.	5-45	11-23d	9-6	11-26
4-55	11-10	8-43	11-10	35	Selly Oak and Navigation St.	5-18	11-30	9-6	11-30
5-3	11-6	8-48	11-6	78	Sho.t Heath and Steelhouse Lane.	5-26	11-30	9-13	11-30
4-56	11-16	8-58	11-16	27	Stafford Road, Handsworth, and Colmore Row.	5-12	11-30	9-13	11-30
4-52	11-6	10-41	11-6	90	Stechford and Seymour Street (via Fazeley Street).	5-18 then 6-50	11-30	10-18	11-30
5-21	11-4	8-48	11-4	84	Stechford and Albert Street (via Deritend).	5-48	11-30	9-13	11-30
5-5	11-8	8-50	11-8	1	Stockland Green and Steelhouse Lane.	5-26	11-30	9-13	11-30
5-7	11-15	8-55	11-15	41	Trafalgar Rd. and Navigation St. (via Leopold St.).	5-26	11-30	9-14	11-30

Above: The date written on the back of this card is 1 April 1939. For a last tram this car is far from full and 1 April was a Saturday, when many revellers might have been expected to board the top deck. This was usually the case with livelier spirits and those who enjoyed a smoke.

Seven

Two 'Cross-Country' Routes

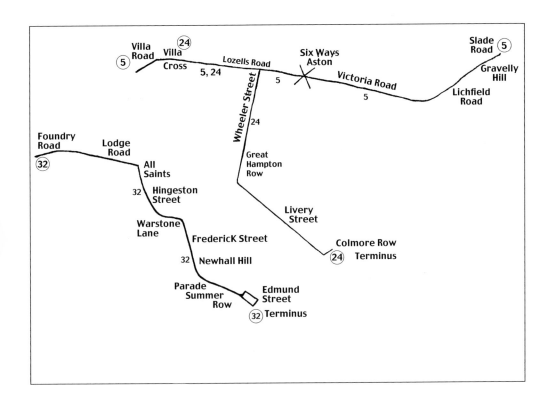

This 32 service made an interesting, weaving-about journey between Lodge Road (see tram window) Winson Green, near the prison, and Edmund Street in the city replete with fine civic buildings and the Arts Faculty, part of the university.

This picture conveys a stereotype image of the traditional prison. The gaol dates back to the mid-nineteenth century, a sort of redbrick castle which quickly became begrimed in the sooty Birmingham atmosphere. The prison has been extensively rebuilt in recent years. A tram route did not pass these grim gates but the outer circle bus did.

Birmingham, The Jewellers Quarter, showing the Chamberlain
Memorial Clock.

The Jewellery Quarter, originating some two hundred years ago in Hockley, is still busily at work today. The Quarter's best known landmark – the cast iron clock tower – stands behind the tram at the junction of Warstone Lane and Vyse Street. The tower commemorated a post-Boer War visit to South Africa in 1903 by Joseph Chamberlain, at the time Secretary of State to the Colonies.

Congreve Street, Birmingham

Along with other services, the 32 travelled down Congreve Street before entering Summer Row. This card was written on 15 October 1912, the traveller voicing complaints about some of her travelling companions: 'It is hot and some swanky people will talk for the benefit of the whole carriage.' (A story as old as communal travel!)

As shown on page 99, the No.5 service set off due east then moved north-east to reach Slade Road, Erdington. In so doing, it travelled through densely populated areas, affording many shopping opportunities 'up Villa Cross', 'on the Lozells', 'at Six Ways'. From the top of his ladder the workman would have a good view of where Villa Road joins Soho Road/Soho Hill.

This is an earlier scene with what appears to be a No.24 at its terminus. This service also ran along Lozells Road but turned right into Wheeler Street on its way to Colmore Row. Sloping away to the right is Heathfield Road, with Barker Street left. A well-stocked milliners seems to have caught the attention of one of the ladies.

On either side of the road stand tempting sources of pleasure, allowing temporary escape from worries and the daily grind. 'Birmingham's Best Beer' is a bold claim but probably successfully alluring. The cinema 'Villa Cross' was a local favourite, not least with the author, while next door H.T. Cross offered Provisions – for sale, see awning.

Saturday 22 October 1938. Went with Eddie to see 'Snow White and 7 dwarf' at Villa + girls late. Had to stand at back of balcony, 6d. Margaret looked sehr schon. We sat down after 1st performance. Snow White great. Terrific, colossal etc. Held Margaret's hand. Very nice.

This card is one of a series to publicise the cinema. On the back it is stated that the card was issued on 22 May 1916 'to celebrate the First Anniversary of this increasingly Popular Picture House.'

The partly hidden garage sign, a driveway to 'round the back' and a double-fronted shop are important indicators of how bicycles and petrol-driven vehicles were making an impact on everyday life. Household names appear: 'Dunlop Tyres 1st in 1888', 'Lucas' and 'Sturmey-Archer' – a noted bicycle gear manufacturer. Next door is a branch of Baines, a local model bakery. But further along, at first floor level, can be seen the three brass balls of a pawnbroker, a sure sign that some local people are living near the breadline.

The road right could be Hartington Road and that left, in front of the car, Berners Street. On the Lozells Road itself, and in the vicinity of the scene shown, was that boon of a shop to a generally impecunious schoolboy, and a few others – one of the many branches of 'Woolies', 'nothing over sixpence'.

Tuesday 4 January 1938. Bought Flying Aces *magazines from Woolworths.* (American aviation magazines.)

One of Birmingham's oldest cinemas, Lozells Picture House opened in 1911. After being rebuilt in 1922, a Wurlitzer organ was installed five years later. Frank Newman became the organist and his regular radio broadcasts during the 1930s were highly popular. The cinema was destroyed during a 1942 air raid.

At this busy junction the No.5 tram (one can be seen in the far distance) passed straight across from Lozells Road into Victoria Road. The policeman on point duty is wearing summer uniform. The corner left, on Birchfield Road, was known locally, and not surprisingly, as 'Atkinson's Corner', a reference to a highly successful chemist.

Victoria Road, Aston.

Aston Baths, the imposing building right, housed two pools. In the late 1920s, sixpence was charged for first-class amenities and fourpence for second. Slipper baths were also available, a blessing within reach of the slightly better off among the many households lacking a bathroom.

By getting off the No.5 near the baths, it would be just a short walk down Upper Thomas Street to Aston Park and Aston Hall in the Park's grounds. This Jacobean mansion dates back to the early seventeenth century. During the English Civil War the Hall was attacked and captured by Roundhead troops. The Hall remains one of Birmingham's historical tourist attractions.

Monday 20 March 1939. A balloon for part of balloon barrage up this dinner-time. Think it is in Aston Park.

Eight

Some City Centre Destinations and Termini

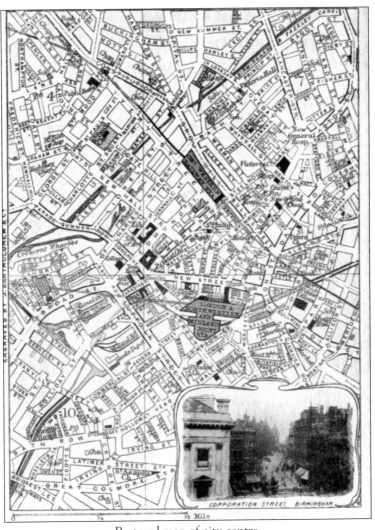

Postcard map of city centre.

This photograph was possibly taken from the Cobden Hotel in Corporation Street. The No.6 tram is about to turn into that street having just picked up passengers at the terminus. On the left is a branch of a world-famous firm – COOKS, with travel posters in its windows. 'Get it at the Beehive in Albert Street' exhorts the tram advert.

A meeting of tram and train services by the GWR main line Snow Hill station. Passengers can be seen boarding the tram which will go left down Snow Hill. A little above and to the left of the Nestles Milk advert (on a tram) is the arched entrance of the Great Western Arcade. The card was posted in 1922.

This view, presumably taken from above ground level in Bull Street or Steelhouse Lane, shows a main line station hotel, typical in its ornateness and grandeur of the Victorian era. The buffet is on the corner of Snow Hill. The station was built on a rather cramped site but was held to be a jewel in the eyes of 'God's Wonderful Railway' buffs.

The nearest tram stands at its Colmore Row sheltered terminus by the railings of St Philip's Anglican Cathedral. That tram service was no longer in operation in 1937. The opening to the right runs into Temple Row. The group of people at the corner may be workers walking (after a tram or bus ride) to work in the many insurance, commercial and banking offices situated in Colmore Row.

This card seems to confirm the doubts of those who opposed one way traffic in some of Birmingham's central streets. The elderly pedestrian, fag in mouth, has a distinct 'I told you so' air about him! The tram, in the thick of things, could be a No.6. Just beyond it stands Lewis's store. The bus seems to be a 1A – for Acocks Green. The card was posted in 1947.

This card was posted forty years earlier, Claude writing on 14 September 1907: 'They have now done away with the traction engines to pull the cars.' Newbury's became Lewis's.

LAW COURTS, BIRMINGHAM.

Queen Victoria laid the foundation stone for what became a suitably magisterial building in 'lower' Corporation Street. A tram track can be seen at the front. The No.6 tram, when heading for Perry Barr, would travel this way, the 'new' fire station being just ahead.

COUNCIL HOUSE, BIRMINGHAM.

Here stands another imposing example of Victorian civic pride and self-confidence. Built between 1874 and 1879, the foundation stone was laid by Joseph Chamberlain, arguably Birmingham's most famous citizen. In adjoining streets were situated municipal offices, e.g. the Education Department in Margaret Street.

Founded by Sir Josiah Mason, industrialist and philanthropist, Mason's College in Edmund Street, the large gothic-style building behind the square, was granted university status in 1900. The rounded corner building opposite was the city's principal public library. Just round the corner in Congreve Street, the Tramway and Omnibus Department had its head office.

Friday 14 June 1940. Stap me, Paris has fallen...Went up to University, Edmund Street, in afternoon, with John and Syd for Oral Examination in French. (The names of those two close friends appear on the school's Roll of Honour.)

The horse and cart are entering Congreve Street from Edmund Street as is the tram. Just beyond the bridge, and right, a series of tram destination boards can be seen. The first in line reads: 'cars load here for Windmill Lane.' This meant service No.30 – Cape Hill (rush periods only).

No doubt many of the people gathered by the Hall of Memory would have travelled into town by tram. Just seven years on from the end of the First World War, painful memories of killed or wounded loved ones would still be raw. Everywhere a two minutes silence would be observed.

Football grounds aside, the Bull Ring was probably the most popular spot in the city for tram age Brummies. The large building on the left, two stone columns marking its entrance, was the Market Hall. Nelson's statue can just be made out near the left-hand column. The tram moving into Digbeth is a No.19, no longer running in 1937.

Designed to accommodate some 600 stalls, the Market Hall dates back to 1835. In this section of the hall the emphasis is clearly on fruit, vegetables and flowers. Sadly, this highly colourful and vibrant sector of the city fell victim to the Blitz.

Monday 26 August 1940. Market Hall has been burned to the ground, only skeleton remaining.

Lewis's regarded itself as the flagship of Birmingham's departmental stores. In any event, it advertised itself as being '200 shops in one…goods & services to satisfy every need' including a bank and post office, hairdressing and beauty services, commonplace today but in 1936, when this card was posted, still something of an exciting novelty.

City Arcade, Birmingham. 649

The city's arcades served a number of purposes: safe short cuts from one busy main street to another, dodging a heavy shower, idling, window shopping and, of course, really shopping. The bowler-hatted man seems particularly taken with the child's tricycle, a good present for a son, daughter or grandchild.

This No.6 car is waiting its turn to move up Martineau Street. Behind the tram, in High Street, is the small but cosy News Theatre, a cinema offering 'The Show That Is Different'. Indeed it was, the programme consisting of newsreels, cartoons and travel films. Converted from a conventional cinema in 1932, the 'theatre' closed in 1960. The photograph was taken in April 1948.

They don't build them like this anymore! A fine example in cast iron and glass of Victorian dignity and durability expressed in street furniture. Built on an island, trams could approach the sheltering passengers from either side. The destinations of the various services are just legible beneath the 'Cars load…' sign.

Sprinting ability was sometimes useful when trying to board a tram. This photograph, taken on 30 August 1938, shows the Edmund Street terminus where cars loaded for Bearwood (29), Oldbury (86) and Dudley (87). The 85 is not listed in the 1937 timetable. The rather ornate bridge links the council house/art gallery-museum to the art gallery's extension.

Nine

Out of the Ordinary

When King Edward VII and Queen Alexandra visited Birmingham on 7 July 1909, the decorated tram formed part of the celebrations. The occasion for the royal visit was the opening of the new redbrick university on Bristol Road, Edgbaston.

Whatever the rights or wrongs of the so-called General Strike of 1926, there can be no doubt that many people remained out of work and very hard-up. The city's Lord Mayor organised what was, in effect, a 'whip round' for the economic casualties. This illuminated tram ran on various Aston routes during 1927/1928 to publicise the appeal.

Electric trams were in their infancy when this accident occurred, a disaster apparently due to total brake failure. Several top deck passengers tried to leap to safety as the tram careered out of control. As can be seen, the tram had been making for Edmund Street from Lodge Road, Winson Green, route 32 in 1937. This card was posted on 18 October 1907.

The struggle to raise the damaged tram to an upright position was clearly very manual labour intensive. Many workmen of the day wore flat caps and waistcoats as shown here. Presumably, given the basic wooden structure, left, the tram was hoisted in a series of short lifts while baulks of timber were wedged against the side of the tram. The operation obviously attracted great public interest.

A handwritten note has been made on both sides of this card: 'Birmingham Tramway funeral likely of victim of first accident. Tram overturned on Lodge Road Route 1-10-1907.'

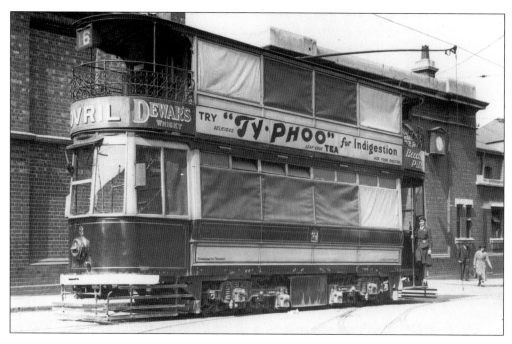

'We just carried on', might well have been the comment of the smartly uniformed 'clippie' on this Perry Barr tram. A similar card states: 'In the raid of April 9/10 1941, 24 cars were destroyed in Miller Street depot and all others lost glass till supply of glass available, patched up as shown.' An official account (1940-1941) states that air raids severely damaged '70 different points and the overhead work proved to be most vulnerable to blast...41 tramcars were completely destroyed...'

One picture that is entirely self-explanatory.

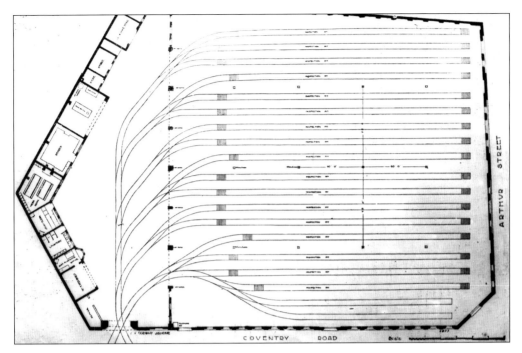

'Coventry Road' and 'Arthur Street' tell us that this is the layout of the depot near St Andrew's, home of Birmingham FC. Between each set of tracks, except the bottom two, appears 'Inspection' and a series of short parallel lines presumably indicating steps down into inspection and repair pits.

This card has been identified on the back as 'Small Heath Depot', the plan for which has been given on the previous card. Some of the cars carry commercial adverts while others do not. But no prizes for guessing that 'rd's ackers' signifies 'Crawford's Cream Crackers'!

This 1938 photograph shows part of the Hockley (Miller Street) Depot. Built in 1904, the depot could house just over 100 cars. Opposite the depot, on the north side of Miller Street, stood the main service yard for the city's tramway system.

Mechanics at work in 1911 in Witton Lane Tram Sheds, Aston. Here the inspection pits, referred to on the previous page, can be seen.

The height of this mobile working platform suggests that it came into use, even though of only one horsepower, in the post-steam, post-cable car period.

A photograph from 1952 in Pebble Mill Road probably forty years after the horse-drawn vehicle had been used. While the basic scaffolding-type structure of the work platform has changed little, the vehicle and its power unit have changed dramatically. Service 36 ran between Cotteridge and Navigation Street.

Compared to the wooden garden seat-type of seating of the early tramway days, (see page 9) what is shown here is relatively plush and reasonably comfortable. Coat after coat of varnish seems to have been applied to sturdy wooden window frames, doors and ceilings. There was nothing flimsy or shoddy about a tram. In fact, the whole ambience of a tram was, for me as a passenger, far 'classier', for want of a better word, than that of fumes-emitting buses.

On the back of this card appears: 'Mr Woodman in Instruction School Moseley Depot.' Conceivably, Mr Woodman is the one man not wearing a uniform. On the bench, left, is a partly stripped down controller with its one large and one small handle.

The Maley Brake Applied to a Bogie Truck

Here is a reminder of the importance of bogies, essential to all carriages, including tram cars, which need to travel around bends. Apparently 'bogie' derives from an old north country word. The first trams to be introduced by the Corporation, in 1904, came to be known as 'old bogies'.

Man at work – somewhat dangerously! This photograph was taken in a West Smethwick depot, the tram apparently belonging to the Dudley and Stourbridge system.

125

The date and location of this photograph of parts of a tram's 'innards' including the uncovered controller, right, are not known. The metal staircase, however, is highly evocative. Workers in thick boots would make quite a clatter as they went up and a greater clatter still as they came down the iron steps. The tram might well lurch and sway prompting wild grabs at the central pole shown.

The ghost town atmosphere of a disused tram track and dreary-looking industrial buildings near Bordesley Station in May 1951 seems to signal the impending disappearance of trams which followed just over two years later.

B'HAM TRAMWAYMEN'S CHURCH PARADE, MAY 16TH, 1909.   H.M.

During the first four decades of the last century, Sunday morning church parades were a common feature of everyday life. All manner of organisations, official and voluntary, such as the boy scouts, marched to church on designated Sundays. These tramwaymen are marching down New Street probably making their way to St Martin's in the Bull Ring. Their assembly point had probably been in front of the Council House in Colmore Row.

28 June 1953, when this photograph was taken, fell on a Sunday. That fact, together with the group of three special trams carrying youngish men, some with cameras, suggest that this was a special trip laid on for tram enthusiasts before the tramway system finished completely on the following Saturday. Presumably a terminus had been reached, probably one of the north-easterly routes in the Erdington direction, these being the last six to be shut down.

The six routes, mentioned on the previous page, consisted of: 1, city to Stockland Green; 2, city to Erdington; 63, city to Tyburn Road; 64, city to High Street, Erdington; 78, city to Short Heath and 79, city to Pype Hayes Park. Here is the 78 on its way along Victoria Road, Aston on the last day of its travels; Saturday 4 July 1953. The interest of the crowd, of all ages, is remarkable. Their spirits had no doubt been raised by the recent coronation of Queen Elizabeth II and the first successful ascent of Mount Everest.

Here is the last official car, No.616 of the Erdington 2 service, at much the same spot in Victoria Road. On that day, 4 July 1953, the *Birmingham Mail* devoted the greater part of its front page to the theme of 'the end of the line', including five photographs. Birmingham's tramways had served the Birmingham public well – in peace, through two world wars and, in all weathers, a worthy history of duties well done and rightful of civic pride. 'Pass along the car please'.